BOYS and GIRLS
Can Live For Jesus

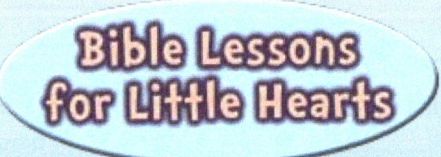

Bible Lessons for Little Hearts

Hlelolwenkhosi Mamba
Illustrations by RKS Illustrations

Boys and Girls Can Live for Jesus:
Bible Lessons For Little Hearts

Copyright © by Hlelolwenkhosi Mamba. All rights reserved. No portion of this book may be reproduced, stored in a retrieval system, or transmitted in any form or by any means, except for brief quotations in printed reviews, without prior permission from the publisher. Requests for information should be addressed to:
Hlelolwenkhosi Mamba
P.O. Box 487
Nhlangano
Swaziland

Or emailed to:
simphiwemamba@gmail.com

Unless otherwise stated, Scripture is taken from the New King James Version (NKJV)®. Copyright © 1982 by Thomas and Nelson. Used by permission. All rights reserved.

Also used: The Holy Bible, New International Version (NIV), copyright © 1973, 1978, 1984 by International Bible Society.

Edited by ChristianEditingServices.com

ISBN: 978-1-928325-69-7

Illustrations by RKS Illustrations
An illustrations, art and design services providing centre of the award winning illustrator, Richa Kinra Shekhar has hundreds of books to her credit. To see her works and styles, visit www.rksillustrations.com.

To my nephew SimeNkhosini. Sonny, you will grow in the fear of the Lord and become everything that God had in mind when He fashioned you in your mother's womb. You will grow to become a man of integrity and live for Jesus. You bring me so much joy. I love you!

Who is Jesus?

Jesus is the Son of God. We can read about Him in the Bible. God sent Jesus to earth as a baby. He was born to Mary and Joseph in a stable in a little town called Bethlehem. He was sent down from heaven to save us from our sins because they had separated us from God. Jesus was willing to come because He loves us so much.

Scripture Reference:

Luke 1:35
And the angel answered and said to her, "The Holy Spirit will come upon you, and the power of the Highest will overshadow you; therefore, also, that Holy One who is to be born will be called the Son of God."

What did Jesus do for me?

If we are honest with ourselves and God, we must admit we have done some bad things. We have told lies, cheated, had a bad attitude, started a fight, been jealous, disobeyed our parents, and maybe even stolen something. These wrong things are called sins. Every person ever born, except Jesus, has sinned. He was perfect, but we are not. Everyone who sins deserves to be punished, but Jesus loved us so much He took our punishment for us. When He was thirty-three years old, He died on a cross. Soldiers pounded nails in His hands and feet. They placed a crown of thorns on His head and pierced His side with a sword. The blood Jesus shed on the cross has great power. It can forgive and cleanse us of our sins. His body was broken so our souls can be whole. He died in our place so we can be free from the guilt of sin and live with Him forever one day in heaven. We should have been crucified, but Jesus took our place. Three days after His death He rose from the dead. He lives today and wants to live inside each of our hearts.

Scripture Reference

1 John 1:8
If we say that we have no sin, we deceive ourselves, and the truth is not in us.

Romans 4:25 (NIV)
He was delivered over to death for our sins and was raised to life for our justification.

Why should I live for Him?
There is nobody in the whole world who loves us as much as Jesus. He willingly gave His life and shed His blood so our sins could be forgiven. He wants only what is best for us. We can always trust Him. When we love Jesus and obey the teachings in His Word, the Bible, His blessings are on our life. This doesn't mean everything will always go the way we want it to, but it does mean He is always with us and will never leave us to face problems alone. We do not have to fret or worry about anything because He promises to take care of us. The best thing we can do is live for Jesus. We will never be sorry we did.

Scripture reference

2 Corinthians 5:15
And He died for all, that those who live should live no longer for themselves, but for Him who died for them and rose again.

How can I live for Him?
You might wonder how you can live for Jesus, and what are some ways you can show your love for Him. In the following pages are a few suggestions to help you grow in your walk with the Lord.

Give Him your heart

Since Jesus proved His love for us by dying for us, we should show Him we love Him by wholly giving our hearts to Him. We do this by admitting we have done wrong and need our sins forgiven. When we believe in our hearts that Jesus died for our sins and rose again from the dead for our salvation, our prayer might sound something like this,

"Lord Jesus, I admit I do wrong things and I am sorry. Thank You for dying on the cross for me. Wash me in Your blood. Come into my heart. I give my life to You. Amen."

When we pray and ask Jesus to forgive us of our sins, He does just that. We are born into His family. He forgives and cleanses us from our sins and becomes our personal Savior.

Scripture reference

1 John 1:9
If we confess our sins, He is faithful and just to forgive us our sins and to cleanse us from all unrighteousness.

Romans 10:9 – 10
That if you confess with your mouth the Lord Jesus and believe in your heart that God has raised Him from the dead, you will be saved. For with the heart one believes unto righteousness and with the mouth confession is made unto salvation.

Share the Good News

Once Jesus becomes our personal Savior, we have a responsibility to share the good news of salvation with others. We feel so blessed to know Him that we can't keep it to ourselves. Everyone needs to hear what Jesus did and what He can do in their lives. This is what the Bible teaches us to do—go and tell others about Jesus and His love for them. We should share with everyone who will listen. We can tell them Jesus loves them and He wants to forgive their sins, just as He forgave ours. We can assure them that if they will give their hearts to Jesus, when they die, He will take them to live with Him in heaven forever.

Scripture reference:

Mark 16:15

And He said to them, "Go into all the world and preach the gospel to every creature."

Spend time with Jesus in prayer and His Word

Just as our bodies need food and water to survive, our souls need spiritual food to be healthy. We need to talk to Jesus, and He will speak to us. We talk to Him through prayer. He speaks to us through His Word. Praying and reading the Bible help us live for Jesus. We can talk to Jesus anywhere and anytime. Some people enjoy talking to Him when they get up in the morning and before they go to sleep at night. It doesn't matter when we talk to Him. He is always willing to listen to us. We can bow our heads and thank Him for the food He has provided. When we spend time with Him in prayer and study the Bible, we will get to know Him better. When we know Him better, we will trust Him more.

Scripture reference:

1 Peter 2:2
As newborn babes, desire the pure milk
of the word that you may grow thereby.

Colossians 4:2
Continue earnestly in prayer, being vigilant in it with thanksgiving.

Honor Him with your body

Jesus willingly allowed His body to be beaten and crucified so our souls could be saved. He gave His all for us. In return, He wants us to offer our bodies as a living sacrifice for Him. He wants to use our hands to help our neighbors and our feet to follow in His footsteps. It pleases Him when we use our eyes to read God's Word and our ears to listen to His voice. We were born to love and serve Him. If we desire to live for Jesus, we need to honor Him with every part of our bodies. When Jesus comes to live inside our hearts, our bodies become a temple of His Holy Spirit. We can honor Jesus with our:

Hands—by not taking what doesn't belong to us without permission.

Mouth—by bridling our tongues and not lying, cursing, or speaking in an unwholesome way.

Eyes—by not watching any immoral television programs.

Ears—by not listening to music that doesn't glorify Jesus.

Feet—by being faithful to attend church.

Scripture reference

1 Corinthians 6:19 - 20 (NIV)

Do you not know that your bodies are temples of the Holy Spirit, who is in you, whom you have received from God? You are not your own; you were bought at a price. Therefore honor God with your bodies.

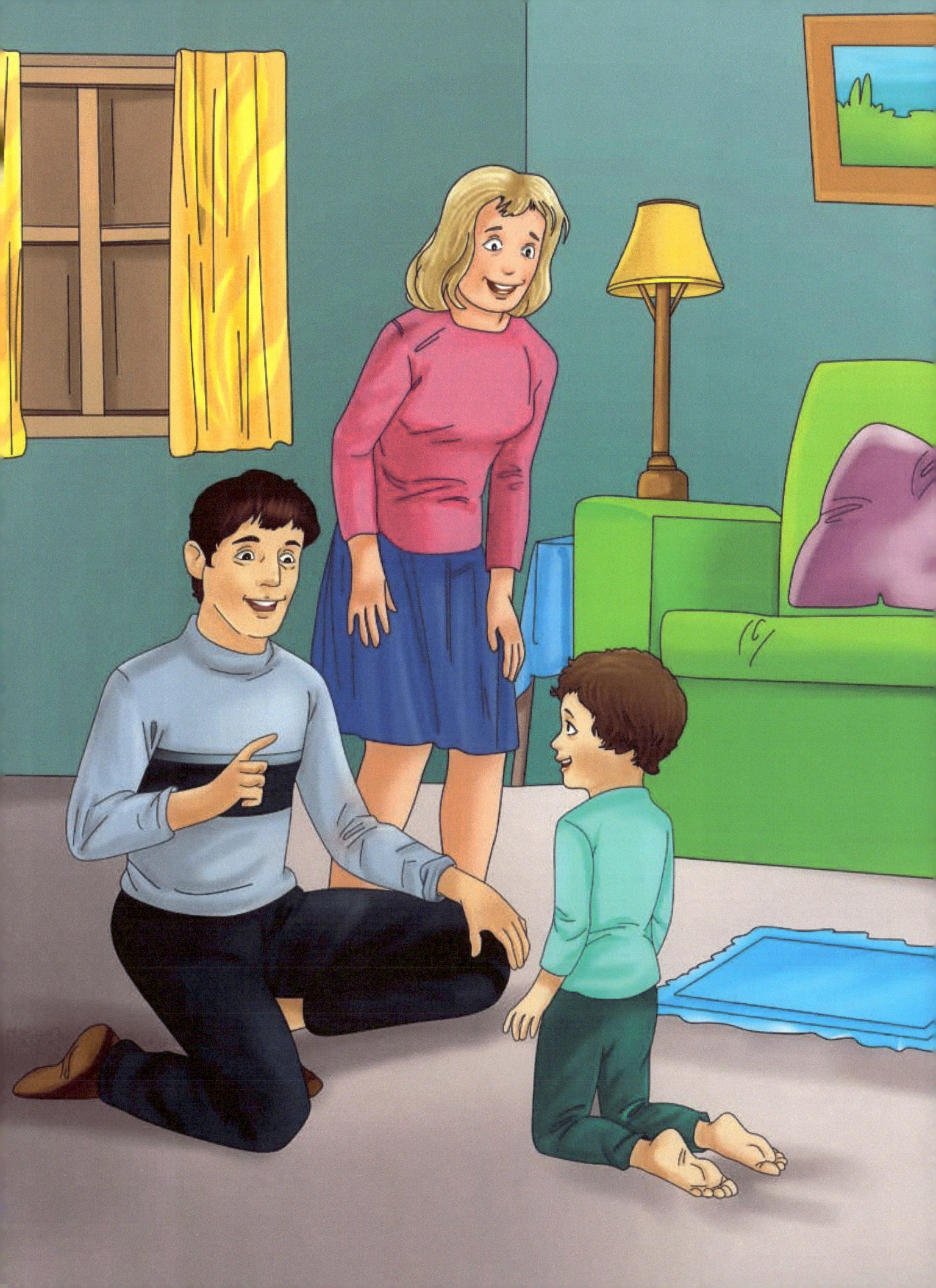

Obey your parents

We can live for Jesus by obeying our parents. It makes Jesus happy when we show respect and honor to our parents. The Bible instructs us to do this. Doing what God's Word commands us pleases Jesus our Lord. If we disobey, we hurt His name. Jesus has placed our parents over us as a covering. We should listen to what they are trying to teach us and promptly obey them with a joyful heart. We should be happy to run errands for them and never talk back at them. We should always speak to them with honor and respect and never throw a temper tantrum if they don't give us what we want. If we do disobey them, we need to quickly apologize to them and ask Jesus to forgive us. It is very important to make our wrongs right. This is an important part of living for Jesus.

Scripture reference

Colossians 3:20
Children, obey your parents in all things
for this is well pleasing to the Lord.

Deuteronomy 5:16
Honor your father and your mother, as the Lord your
God has commanded you, that your days may
be long, and that it may be well with you…

Love your neighbors

Our neighbors are not only the people who live close to our house but also every person we come in contact with. If we live for Jesus, we love other people as we love ourselves. Some of them may not love us back and may even be rude, but that's not our problem. We shouldn't worry about how they act. We must be concerned about our actions. We must play our part, which is to love them no matter how they act toward us and then leave the rest with Jesus. He will take care of it. When we love other people, we show Jesus that we love Him and we live for Him. Obeying this command of the Bible pleases the Lord.

Scripture reference

Mark 12:30 – 31

'And you shall love the Lord your God with all your heart, with all your soul, with all your mind, and with all your strength.' This is the first commandment. "And the second, like it, is this, 'You shall love your neighbor as yourself.' there is no other commandment greater than these."

1 John 2:9

He who says he is in the light, and hates his brother, is in darkness until now.

Be generous to others

We live for Jesus by sharing what we have with others who may not have very much. The Lord loves a cheerful, generous giver. When we are generous to others, Jesus is pleased.

Scripture reference

Hebrews 13:16
But do not forget to do good and to share, for with such sacrifices God is well pleased.

Luke 6:38
Give, and it will be given to you; good measure, pressed down, shaken together, and running over will be put into your bosom. For with the same measure that you use, it will be measured back to you.

Luke 3:11
He answered and said to them, "He who has two tunics, let him give to him who has none; and he who has food let him do likewise.

Forgive those who have wronged you

It doesn't take long in this life to discover that sometimes we offend others and other times they offend us. When someone wrongs us, we need to sincerely forgive them as soon as possible. When we forgive those who have wronged us, we show that we love Jesus and live for Him. He is pleased when we forgive others. He also forgives us our own sins if we forgive others the wrongs they do to us. When we wrong others, we need to be humble enough to ask for forgiveness. "I'm sorry" will always be two of the greatest words we can say.

Scripture reference

Ephesians 4:32
And be kind to one another, tenderhearted, forgiving one another, even as God in Christ forgave you.

Matthew 6:14 – 15 (NIV)
For if you forgive other people when they sin against you, your heavenly Father will also forgive you. But if you do not forgive others their sins, your Father will not forgive your sins.

Choose good friends

We will become like the people we run around with. We need to choose our friends wisely. There are only two types of friends—good friends and bad friends. Good friends encourage us to be a better person. Bad friends don't have our best interests in mind. They care only about what benefits them. We live for Jesus by choosing good friends and also by being a good friend.

Actions of good friends	Actions of bad friends
They are loving and kind to others	They are rude and bully others
They share their toys with other children	They are selfish and want to keep all the toys to themselves
They encourage us to ask if we need something	They encourage us to steal to get something we want
They listen to and are respectful to elders	They refuse to take instructions from elders and demand their way
They always encourage us to do good things	They mislead us, encouraging us to misbehave
They are generous towards others	They are stingy and not willing to share what they have with others

Scripture reference:

1 Corinthians 15:33
Do not be deceived: "Evil company corrupts good habits."

2 Corinthians 6:14 (NIV)
Do not be yoked together with unbelievers. For what do righteousness and wickedness have in common? Or what fellowship can light have with darkness?

www.ingramcontent.com/pod-product-compliance
Lightning Source LLC
Chambersburg PA
CBHW042127040426
42450CB00002B/104